3-D THRILLERS!

REPTILES

PAUL HARRISON

Capella

What is a

What do you think of when you hear the words *reptile* or *amphibian*? Many people think of cold, slimy snakes, but they couldn't be more wrong. True, snakes are reptiles, but they are nothing like you might imagine, and they are just one member of the extended reptile clan. There are over seven thousand types of reptile and way more than four thousand kinds of amphibian all of which come in lots of shapes and sizes, from giant lizards and huge tortoises to the tiniest of frogs.

MEET THE ANCESTORS

Reptiles, impressive as they are, just aren't what they used to be. Even the biggest of today's lizards don't match up to their huge predecessors, the dinosaurs. That's right; those mighty monsters from the past were all reptiles, too. So the next time a snake gives you the shivers or a turtle gives you a fright, be thankful it isn't a T. rex instead. In fact, reptiles were around long before the dinosaurs appeared. The oldest fossil reptile found so far is over 340 million years old. And amphibians are even older – some fossils date back over 360 million years.

Reptile?

BIG AND SMALL

Even though today's reptiles aren't as big as before, they still cover a wide range of sizes. Anacondas, giant South American snakes, can grow up to between 8 and 11 metres in length – that's about the length of two and a half family cars. At the other end of the scale, the smallest reptiles are geckos. Some don't grow any longer than around 2.5 centimetres.

People who study reptiles are called *herpetologists*.

SUN LOVERS

Reptiles can be found virtually anywhere, whether it's in a high-rise in Los Angeles, a desert in Africa, or even in the depths of the Indian Ocean. But you'll not find one in most Arctic areas or in Antarctica. That's due to the fact that reptiles don't like the cold, so you'll never bump into one on a ski slope!

Body Bits

So, what makes a reptile what it is? Although they may look very different from each other, all reptiles have some things in common — even if it doesn't seem like it at first.

NOT GOOD IN THE MORNING

Reptiles are often called cold-blooded, which means they can't generate their own body heat. Instead, reptiles have to rely on the sun to warm them up. Reptiles are very sluggish when they haven't warmed up enough, which makes it easy for predators to catch them. The warmer it is, the quicker reptiles warm up, which is why reptiles don't live in cold areas.

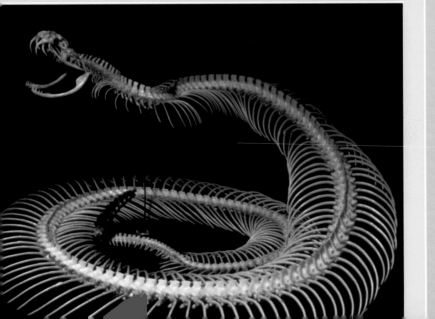

BITS AND PIECES

All reptiles have a skeleton with a backbone and lay eggs, which have a waterproof shell. Remarkably, reptiles all either have four legs or had ancestors which had four legs – this also includes snakes. Of course, snakes lost their legs a long time ago, but their ancestors had them and you can still see small traces of legs on some snakes' skeletons.

SCALES

All reptiles have scales, which are made from *keratin* – the same stuff your fingernails are made from. Their skin is also very dry as it is specially designed to stop reptiles from losing water from their bodies. On some reptiles, such as crocodiles, the scales fuse together to form plates, which makes the skin tougher.

Reptiles can virtually shut their bodies down if they get too cold.

GOING UP

Reptiles are great climbers and this is due to their special feet. Reptiles have clawed feet, which are an obvious help. But some lizards, such as geckos, have an added advantage with millions of little hairs, called 'setae', on the bottom of their feet. These tiny hairs allow geckos to climb walls with the greatest of ease. Other reptiles rely on extra-grippy tails to help them balance on branches.

Here be Dra

When people first found fossils they imagined they must be the bones of monsters or dragons. Then, when explorers and traders went to foreign climates and saw some of the biggest and most fearsome-looking reptiles, they came back with even taller tales of gigantic beasts. Although these creatures were bigger in the imagination than in reality, these modern-day monsters are still impressive creatures.

It was once believed that a stare from a basilisk lizard was enough to kill you!

WORTH MONITORING

The heavyweights of the lizard world are the monitors, and king amongst them is the Komodo dragon. Found only on the island of Komodo and some neighbouring islands, these fearsome creatures grow to over 3 metres and weigh more than two people put together. They are big enough to kill and eat deer and have even been known to eat children!

gons

PROUD PARENTS

A crocodile might be the last thing you want to see when you're going for a swim, but as far as their babies are concerned, they're great parents. Crocodiles are one of the few members of the reptile family who take care of their young. They build or dig nests for their eggs and, when they hatch, the crocodile is there to take care of its new brood. Indeed, some species even carry their babies from the nest to the water edge in their mouth – and aren't tempted to eat a single one!

SNEAKY SNAPPER

There are over 20 species of *crocodilian*, including crocodiles, alligators, and *caimans*. The biggest are saltwater crocodiles which can grow to over 6 metres long and weigh more than a car. Crocodilians are very good at hiding in the water – even the big ones – and ambush their prey, sneaking up on them as they drink before lunging out of the water to grab them. In fact, some species of crocodile can even jump straight up out of the water.

NOT A PRETTY SIGHT

The marine iguana is so odd-looking that even the renowned naturalist Charles Darwin described them as "disgusting". However, he was probably impressed by their swimming skills as this strange lizard can stay underwater for up to an hour.

Snakes Alive

Right at the top of the list of things which people are scared of are snakes. Most people with a snake phobia have never seen a snake, and it's fair to say that they get a bad rap. In reality, snakes aren't at all like you'd imagine. They're very shy animals and are much happier scurrying away from people than attacking them. Many snakes are harmless anyway, and even the most poisonous ones will only bite if provoked or surprised.

FANG-TASTIC

Poisonous snakes don't have the biggest fangs you're likely to see in the animal kingdom, but they're very effective at what they do. Like hypodermic needles, snakes' fangs are perfect for injecting poison into their prey.

Some snakes, such as rattlesnakes even have movable fangs which fold back into the roof of the mouth when they're not needed.

HOODED KING

Some of the world's snakes are *venomous*, which means they inject poison into their prey when they bite them. By far the most famous venomous snake is the cobra with its distinctive hood of skin behind its head. The largest of the cobra family is the king cobra, which is so venomous that it can kill an elephant with a single bite.

OPEN WIDE

Swallowing your food down whole without chewing it may sound like terrible table manners, but it's exactly what snakes do. Snakes have fangs but no teeth for chewing; instead they have very flexible jaws. When it comes to meal times, snakes open their mouths as wide as possible and swallow their prey whole – always head first, as it's easier to swallow that way.

BIG SQUEEZE

The biggest snakes are the *constrictors* – snakes like pythons and boas which crush their prey to death by wrapping them in their coils and squeezing really tightly. The largest snakes of all are anacondas, which live in rivers in South America.

Over 7,000 people are bitten by snakes in America every year. Luckily, very few cases prove fatal.

Hard Shell

You might know them as slow-moving lettuce chompers, and it's true that often tortoises and turtles don't seem in much of a hurry, but the *chelonian* family includes some truly remarkable animals. Some species travel thousands of kilometres across the oceans, others can live longer than practically any other animal on earth. Take a peek under the shell of the chelonians and meet the truly terrific tortoises, turtles and terrapins.

HARD CASE

All members of the chelonian family have a shell. The shell is part of the turtles' skeleton and is generally very hard and protective. The top of a turtle shell is called the carapace and the bottom is called the plastron. Some chelonians can even bring their legs, head and tail into the shell for extra protection. But not all chelonian shells are hard. The leatherback turtle, for example, has a soft shell. This is because this turtle swims to great depths in the sea where the water pressure would otherwise crack it.

WHAT'S WHAT?

All chelonians are turtles, but people tend to call different ones different names. As a general rule of thumb, a tortoise lives on land and a turtle lives in the water. In the UK, a turtle that lives in freshwater is called a terrapin.

FLIPPING BRILLIANT

There are over 250 species of turtles and tortoises, and many of them spend their time in water. Only seven species of turtle spend all their time in the ocean. These sea turtles, like this loggerhead turtle, have large flippers instead of legs to help them swim, and only come on land to lay their eggs.

UNDER THREAT

Like many members of the reptile and amphibian families, turtles are under threat. Loss of habitat, hunting, poaching and pollution are slowly killing off some species of these ancient, stately creatures. In some countries, it is now illegal to have a tortoise as a pet unless it has been born in the same country.

GENTLE GIANTS

Some of the most famous tortoises of all are those found on the Galapagos Islands of the Pacific Ocean. These giants can measure over 1 metre from head to tail and weigh over 200 kilograms. Even more remarkably, these gentle giants can live for between 150 and 200 years.

When people talk about reptiles they often mean amphibians as well. In fact, amphibians are entirely different creatures, but just as amazing. The easiest way to tell them apart is to look at the skin. All reptiles have scales, but amphibians don't. Amphibian skin is much thinner than reptile skin, and amphibians also lose moisture through their skin, which is why they live in water or damp environments.

DON'T TOUCH

Some amphibians aren't quick enough to escape predators, so they've come up with a clever way of protecting themselves – they poison their attackers! When threatened, the amphibians ooze poison from their skin, which not only tastes bad but could possibly kill some predators.

SURPRISE SURPRISE

Even though frogs and toads prefer warm, damp conditions you'd be surprised where they turn up. They don't all live by the sides of ponds – you'll find them in trees in the rainforests of South America and even in the deserts of Australia. These desert-living frogs spend much of their time buried underground waiting for the rain to return.

ders

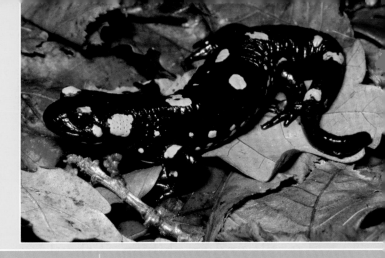

FROG OR TOAD?

How can you tell the difference between a frog and a toad? Look at the skin – if it's smooth it's a frog, if bumpy it's probably a toad.

FOND OF FIRE?

Salamanders are secretive creatures, often confused with lizards. Many old wives tales grew up about these retiring amphibians, the most famous one being that they could not be harmed by fire. This, of course, is absolute nonsense. Perhaps someone threw a log where a salamander was hiding onto a fire and spotted it scurrying away. Who knows?

NEWT NEWS

Newts are part of the salamander family. Some newts live on the land and others in the water, but like many amphibians, they all breed in water. Young newts live on land for the first 2 years and then return to the water to breed or to live permanently.

SQUIRMY WORMY

Is it a snake? Is it an eel? Is it a worm? No – it's a *caecilian*. These blind, legless amphibians spend most of their lives underground and use their sense of smell to find their food.

You can't get warts from handling toads!

Frills and

W ith so many different types of reptile and amphibian, it should come as no surprise that some of them look a little odd. And sometimes their behaviour is just as strange, too.

TREE HOPPER

You can find reptiles everywhere – under the ground, up trees, on the water, in the water and even in the air. Some tree-dwelling lizards have taken to springing into the air to reach trees that are too far away to reach. Although called flying dragons, these reptiles in fact use special flaps of skin to help them glide, like a hang-glider, from tree to tree.

WALKING ON WATER

If a basilisk lizard is in a hurry and there's water in its path, the lizard won't go round it or swim across it. Instead, it picks up speed and runs over the top of it on two legs. This miraculous behaviour earned it the name the Jesus lizard.

BUG EYED MARVEL

The chameleon is a remarkable beast. Not only does it have poppy-out eyes which can move in opposite directions to each other and a long tongue which can shoot out to catch flies, it can also change colour. It is often thought that chameleons change colour to blend into their background, but some scientists believe the colour change happens to show when a chameleon is angry or feels threatened.

Spills

PARENTS WITH POUCHES

Some frogs and toads go to extraordinary lengths to take care of their eggs and young. The Suriname toad actually carries her eggs around on her back, where they sit embedded into her skin. Some frogs have pouches like kangaroos where their young can grow up in safety. Unsurprisingly, these amphibians are known as marsupial frogs.

Some lizards' tails snap off if they're captured so they can escape. The tail grows back, but not as long as before.

PUTTING ON A SHOW

If reptiles feel threatened, the first thing they do is try to get away. This is true of the tiniest gecko and of the largest alligator or snake. If reptiles get cornered, however, they have different ways of reacting. Some reptiles will play dead, rattlesnakes will shake the tip of their tails to produce a rattling noise as a warning, but one of the most startling of displays comes from the frilled lizard of Australia. This lizard will spread out a frill around its head and hiss at the animal chasing it. The frill makes the lizard look much bigger than it is and, hopefully, puts off the attacker.

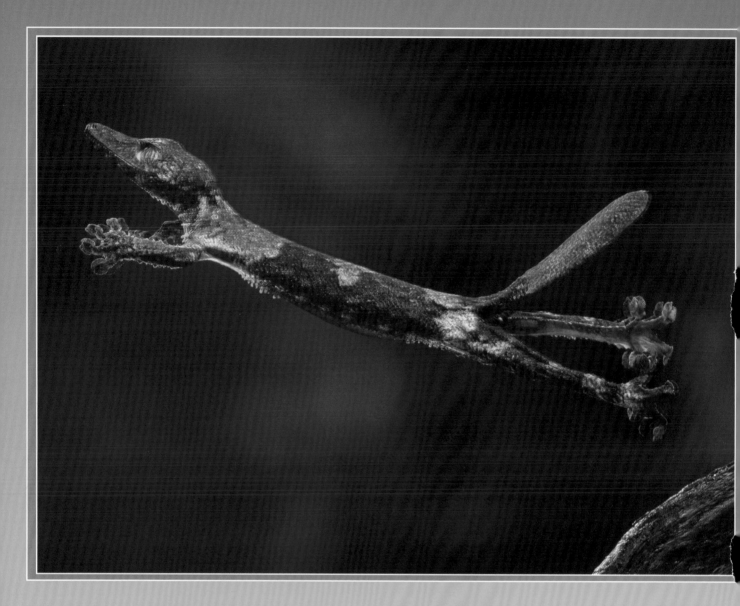

This edition published in 2008 by Arcturus Publishing Limited
26/27 Bickels Yard, 151–153 Bermondsey Street,
London SE1 3HA

Author: Paul Harrison
Designer: Ian Thompson
Editor: Rebecca Gerlings

Picture credits:
NHPA Limited: Cover, title page; page 3, middle; page 3, bottom
right; page 5, top; page 5, middle; page 5, bottom; page 6; page 7,
middle; page 7, bottom right; page 9, top right and back cover; page
9, middle; page 10, top; page 10, bottom; page 11, bottom; page
13, middle left; page 14, top right, middle left and middle right;
page 15, top right; page 16.
Oxford Scientific (OSF)/Photolibrary.com: Page 2; page 4, middle;
page 4, bottom left; page 9, bottom right; page 11, middle; page 12,
top; page 12, bottom; page 13, top right; page 13, middle right;
page 15, bottom right.
Science Photo Library: Page 3, top right; page 8; page 13, bottom left.
John White Photos: Page 7, top left.
Nature Picture Library: Page 11, top right.

3-D images by Pinsharp 3D Graphics

Printed in Malaysia

ISBN: 978-1-84193-295-8